the

zen

sayings, parables,
meditations & haiku

david schiller

WORKMAN PUBLISHING · NEW YORK

Copyright © 1994, 2021 by David Schiller
Originally published as *The Little Zen Companion*

All rights reserved. No portion of this book may be reproduced—
mechanically, electronically, or by any other means, including
photocopying—without written permission of the publisher.
Published simultaneously in Canada by Thomas Allen & Son Limited.

Library of Congress Cataloging-in-Publication Data

Names: Schiller, David (Artist), compiler.
Title: The little book of Zen : sayings, parables, meditations & haiku /
    David Schiller.
Other titles: Little Zen companion.
Description: [Second edition] | New York : Workman Publishing Co., Inc.,
    2021.
Identifiers: LCCN 2020055771 | ISBN 9781523512454 (paperback)
Subjects: LCSH: Zen Buddhism--Quotations, maxims, etc. |
    Zen meditations.
Classification: LCC BQ9267 .L56 2021 | DDC 294.3/927—dc23
LC record available at https://lccn.loc.gov/2020055771

ISBN 978-1-5235-1245-4

Design by Janet Vicario

Workman books are available at special discounts when purchased in
bulk for premiums and sales promotions as well as for fundraising or
educational use. Special editions or book excerpts can also be created
to specification. For details, contact the Special Sales Director at
specialmarkets@workman.com.

Workman Publishing Co., Inc.
225 Varick Street
New York, NY 10014-4381
workman.com

WORKMAN is a registered trademark of Workman Publishing Co., Inc.

Printed in the United States of America
First printing July 2021

10 9 8 7 6 5 4 3 2 1

For Quinn, Theo, Clara, and
Eliana, masters for life

The pears are not viols,
nudes or bottles.
They resemble nothing else.

—WALLACE STEVENS

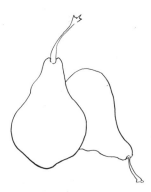

Introduction

ZEN. SUCH AN ELUSIVE LITTLE WORD. These days it's typically used as a synonym for calm. When something is "so zen," it's spare and serene. When someone's in a "zen state," they're relaxed yet focused. It's become shorthand for *mindfulness,* an aspiration for a culture overwhelmed by noise and distraction.

But this is only one facet of Zen and its long and rich tradition. Zen is spiritual. Zen is quirky. It's poetic, earthy, Buddhist yet universal. It is esoteric, almost indefinable, but right there for every person, no matter what they believe in, as a path toward finding real happiness and meaning in life. It is as simple as *When hungry, eat; when tired, sleep.* And as consuming as the lifetime of effort it takes to understand its truths.

This book doesn't presume to explain Zen, but to offer a taste of Zen's way of looking at the world: where the best moment is now, where things are what they seem, and where we see with the refreshing directness of a child rather than through eyes clouded over by routine and judgment. Where the everyday is filled with wonder.

The sayings, poems, dialogues, parables, and stories collected in *The Little Book of Zen* have been chosen for their power to suggest. There are quotes from the very masters who gave Zen its shape and from those who may never have even heard of Zen, yet whose work and life embodies its spirit (Henry David Thoreau, for example). Words on everything from the rigors of practice to making

tea, from art and nature to modern physics and the stars at
night, from the thingness of things to the inexpressible nature
of enlightenment. And many, many words that come with a
wink. Sure, Zen is a matter of life and death. But that doesn't
mean there isn't room for lightness or irreverence.

Words, of course, can never be a substitute for
experience. Reading about fruit just isn't the same as biting
into a peach, which perfectly exemplifies Zen's paradoxical
relationship with language: Its essence is the *wordless*
transmission of truth, yet millions of words have been written
about it, including by its most enlightened teachers. Why?
Give words time to work, including those presented here, and
you might find—not the truth, but a finger pointing the way.

A HISTORICAL NOTE

Zen originated in China in the sixth century BCE as a meeting
of Indian Buddhism with Taoism, merging the speculative with
the practical, the metaphysical with the earthy. Called *Ch'an*
(meditation) in China, it stressed the direct work of sitting over
abstract teaching as the shortest and steepest way to realizing
the Buddha-mind inherent in all of us. Two lines initially
developed: the Northern school of gradual enlightenment
and the eventually dominant Southern school of sudden
enlightenment. Zen reached its Golden Age in the T'ang and
early Sung dynasties (roughly the seventh through the twelfth
centuries) and arrived in Japan about 1190 CE, where the houses
of Soto and Rinzai continue to flourish. The first Zen teachers
came to America around 1905 CE.

In the beginner's mind there are many possibilities, but in the expert's mind there are few.

—SHUNRYŪ SUZUKI

Before a person studies Zen, mountains
are mountains and waters are waters;
after a first glimpse into the truth
of Zen, mountains are no longer
mountains and waters are not waters;
after enlightenment, mountains are
once again mountains and waters once
again waters.

—ZEN SAYING

I'm not young enough to know everything.

—J. M. BARRIE

The birds always find their way to their nests. The river always finds its way to the ocean.

—ZEN PROVERB

We already have everything we need.

—PEMA CHÖDRÖN

Good pitching will always stop good hitting, and vice versa.

—CASEY STENGEL

"I am going to pose a question," King Milinda said to Venerable Nagasena. "Can you answer?"

Nagasena said, "Please ask your question."

The king said, "I have already asked."

Nagasena said, "I have already answered."

The king said, "What did you answer?"

Nagasena said, "What did you ask?"

The king said, "I asked nothing."

Nagasena said, "I answered nothing."

—ZEN MONDO

If you have to ask what jazz is, you'll never know.

—LOUIS ARMSTRONG

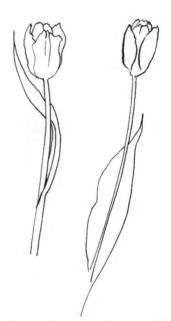

The tao that can be told
is not the eternal Tao.
The name that can be
named is not the eternal
Name.

—*TAO TE CHING*

After taking the high seat to preach to the assembly, Fa-yen raised his hand and pointed to the bamboo blinds. Two monks went over and rolled them up in the same way.

Fa-yen said, "One gains, one loses."

—ZEN KOAN

The thing about Zen is that it pushes
contradictions to their ultimate limit
where one has to choose between
madness and innocence. And Zen
suggests that we may be driving toward
one or the other on a cosmic scale.
Driving toward them because, one way
or the other, as madmen or innocents,
we are already there. It might be good
to open our eyes and see.

—THOMAS MERTON

The Koan

Perhaps no aspect of Zen is as puzzling and yet intriguing to Westerners as the koan. Or as misunderstood. A koan is not a riddle, nor is it a paradox designed to shock the mind. Instead, it is an integral part of a system honed over centuries to help bring the student to a direct realization of ultimate reality.

Taken from the Japanese *ko* ("public") and *an* ("proposition"), the koan can be a question, an excerpt from the sutras, an episode in the life of an ancient Master, a word exchanged in a mondo, or any other fragment of teaching. There are some 1,700 traditional koans in existence.

Koan practice begins when the Master assigns a classic first koan like *Mu*—Chao-chou's reply to the monk who asked him, "Has the dog Buddha-nature or not?" It may literally take years of living with *Mu* before a student truly understands it. But afterward, the next koans—and there may be as many as 500 of them, in five progressive stages—are often "answered" in rapid succession.

The great Japanese Master Hakuin wrote, "If you take up one koan and investigate it unceasingly, your mind will die and your will will be destroyed. It is as though a vast, empty abyss lay before you, with no place to set your hands and feet. You face death and your bosom feels as though it were on fire. Then suddenly you are one with the koan, and body and mind are cast off. . . . This is known as seeing into one's nature."

The bad news is that
you're falling through
air, nothing to hang
on to, no parachute.
The good news is
there's no ground.

—CHÖGYAM TRUNGPA RINPOCHE

Wakuan complained when he saw a picture of bearded Bodhidharma, "Why hasn't that fellow a beard?"

—ZEN KOAN

"But the Emperor has nothing on at all!" cried a little child.

—HANS CHRISTIAN ANDERSEN

One day a man approached Ikkyū and asked: "Master, will you please write for me some maxims of the highest wisdom?"

Ikkyū took his brush and wrote: "Attention."

"Is that all?" asked the man.

Ikkyū then wrote: "Attention. Attention."

"Well," said the man, "I really don't see much depth in what you have written."

Then Ikkyū wrote the same word three times: "Attention. Attention. Attention."

Half-angered, the man demanded: "What does that word 'Attention' mean, anyway?"

Ikkyū gently responded, "Attention means attention."

—ZEN STORY

Attention is the beginning of devotion.

—MARY OLIVER

You can't stop the waves but you can learn to surf.

—JON KABAT-ZINN

As regards the quietude of the sage,
he is not quiet because quietness is
said to be good. He is quiet because
the multitude of things cannot disturb
his quietude. When water is still, one's
beard and eyebrows are reflected in it.
A skilled carpenter uses it in a level to
obtain a measurement. If still water
is so clear, how much more are the
mental faculties! The mind of a sage
is the mirror of heaven and earth in
which all things are reflected.

—CHUANG TZU

Standing on the bare ground . . .
a mean egotism vanishes. I become a
transparent eyeball; I am nothing;
I see all; the currents of the Universal
Being circulate through me; I am part
or particle of God.

—RALPH WALDO EMERSON

Ralph Waldo Emerson once asked what we would do if the stars only came out once every thousand years. No one would sleep that night, of course. The world would create new religions overnight. We would be ecstatic, delirious, made rapturous by the glory of God. Instead, the stars come out every night and we watch television.

—PAUL HAWKEN

There is nothing mystifying about Zen. Zen is clarity itself.

—TAKASHI IKEMOTO

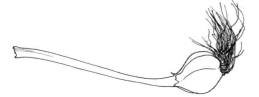

Soon the child's clear eye is clouded
over by ideas and opinions,
preconceptions, and abstractions.
Simple free being becomes encrusted
with the burdensome armor of the ego.
Not until years later does an instinct
come that a vital sense of mystery has
been withdrawn. The sun glints through
the pines, and the heart is pierced in a
moment of beauty and strange pain, like
a memory of paradise. After that day, we
become seekers.

—PETER MATTHIESSEN

Just try to feel your own weight, in your own seat, in your own feet. Okay? So if you can feel that weight in your body, if you can come back into the most personal identification, a very personal identification, which is: I am. This is me now. Here I am, right now. This is me now. Then you don't feel like you have to leave, and be over there, or look over there. You don't feel like you have to rush off and be somewhere.

—BILL MURRAY

If the doors
of perception
were cleansed
everything
would appear
to man as it is,
infinite.

—WILLIAM BLAKE

As I grew up I became increasingly interested in philosophy, of which they [his family] profoundly disapproved. Every time the subject came up they repeated with unfailing regularity, "What is mind? No matter. What is matter? Never mind." After some fifty or sixty repetitions, this remark ceased to amuse me.

—BERTRAND RUSSELL

The eye with which I see God is the same eye with which God sees me.

—MEISTER ECKHART

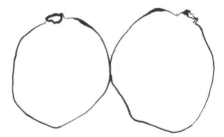

Wherever you are is the entry point.

—KABIR

Ring the bells that still can
   ring.
Forget your perfect offering.
There is a crack in
   everything.
That's how the light gets in.

—LEONARD COHEN

The gaps are the thing. The gaps are
the spirit's one home, the altitudes and
latitudes so dazzlingly spare and clean
that the spirit can discover itself like a
once-blind man unbound. The gaps are
the clefts in the rock where you cower
to see the back parts of God; they are
fissures between mountains and cells the
wind lances through, the icy narrowing
fiords splitting the cliffs of mystery. Go
up into the gaps. If you can find them;
they shift and vanish too. Stalk the gaps.
Squeak into a gap in the soil, turn, and
unlock—more than a maple—a universe.

—ANNIE DILLARD

A monk once asked Yun-men, "What teaching goes beyond the buddhas and patriarchs?"

Yun-men said, "Sesame cake."

Do you feel your hairs standing on end?

—*BLUE CLIFF RECORD*

If you cannot find the truth
right where you are, where else
do you expect to find it?

—DŌGEN

The only Zen
you find on
the tops of
mountains is
the Zen you
bring up there.

—ROBERT M. PIRSIG

What Is Buddha?

Again and again students ask, "What is Buddha?" The Masters' seemingly nonsensical responses have survived over the centuries, often as koans:

> *"Three pounds of flax."*
> —Tung-shan

> *"Dried shitstick."*
> —Yun-men

> *"This very mind."*
> —Ma-tsu

> *"Not mind, not Buddha."*
> —Ma-tsu

> *"What is not the Buddha?"*
> —Nan-yang Hui-chung

> *"The cat is climbing up the post."*
> —Pa-chiao Hui-ch'ing

"I never knew him."
—Nan-yang Hui-chung

"A new bride rides a donkey, the mother-in-law leads it."
—Shou-shan

"When you utter the name of Buddha, wash out your mouth."
—Zen saying

"Look within, thou art Buddha."
—*The Voice of the Silence*

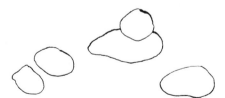

I'm awake; I am in the world—

I expect

no further assurance.

—LOUISE GLÜCK

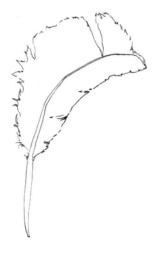

A Zen Vocabulary

KENSHO: self-realization; seeing into one's own nature

JIRIKI: "one's own power," referring to a person's endeavor to attain enlightenment through his or her own efforts

SATORI: a state of intuitive enlightenment, particularly the Enlightenment experienced by the Buddha

BODHISATTVA: an enlightened being who renounces entry into Nirvana until all other beings are saved

Zen is the unsymbolization of the world.

—R. H. BLYTH

I saw somebody peeing in Jermyn Street the other day. I thought, is this the end of civilization as we know it? Or is it simply somebody peeing in Jermyn Street?

—ALAN BENNETT

Rose is a rose is a rose is a rose.

—GERTRUDE STEIN

Things are entirely what they appear to be and behind them . . . there is nothing.

—JEAN-PAUL SARTRE

Living Zen

SITTING

*"Meditation is not about some state
but about the meditator. It's not about some activity,
or about fixing something or about accomplishing
something. It's about ourselves."*

—Charlotte Joko Beck

Zen is in the living. The Masters stress it again and again:
You must walk the path yourself. Which, in the case of
Zen, begins and ends with seated meditation, or *zazen*.
Of course there are many kinds of meditation, but here's
how to get started with *zazen*.

First, decide where and when you will sit. A quiet
corner is best, and most people prefer to meditate early
in the morning or later in the evening, away from the
day's distractions. As for what to sit on, try a firm pillow,
or a chair if you're not used to sitting cross-legged. Or,
order a *zafu*—a proper meditation cushion—from a seller
of meditation supplies.

Next, arrange your body in a stable position, which
begins with the legs. When you see pictures of the Buddha
or experienced monks, they are sitting in a Full Lotus

position—legs crossed with both feet resting atop opposite thighs. But when beginning, the important thing is not how you're sitting, but that you are steady, balanced, and grounded.

Then, moving up the body, follow this Zen saying: *Belly forward, buttocks back*. The belly is relaxed; chest is out; head is up; chin is slightly tucked in; and hands rest on the lap, where you might want to form an oval, or mudra, with your fingers. Keep your eyes open but unfocused on a spot on the floor three or four feet ahead (it helps keep you present and awake!) and mouth closed, with tongue resting against the upper palate (which prevents the distracting accumulation of saliva).

Set a timer, and it doesn't matter how long—another Zen saying: *One minute sitting, one minute Buddha*—and start to breathe with intention. A perfect beginning practice, yet one that will last your whole life, is to count from one to ten, silently sounding each number on the in-breath or out-breath. Chances are you won't get all the way to ten without getting distracted—our monkey mind is too strong. But on the other hand, "getting there" is not the point. It's the sitting, the breathing, the stillness, the effort. And the clear, easeful feeling of being at home.

The thing about meditation is: You become more and more you.

—DAVID LYNCH

The hardest thing, I think, is to live richly in the present, without letting it be tainted & spoiled out of fear for the future or regret for a badly-managed past.

—SYLVIA PLATH

Once Ma-tsu and Pai-chang were walking along and they saw some wild ducks fly by.

"What is that?" the Master asked.

"Wild ducks," Pai-chang replied.

"Where have they gone?"

"They've flown away," Pai-chang said.

The Master then gave Pai-chang's nose a tweak, and when Pai-chang looked startled, Ma-tsu said, "When have they ever flown away?"

—ZEN KOAN

The flower is not red, nor is the willow green.

—ZEN SAYING

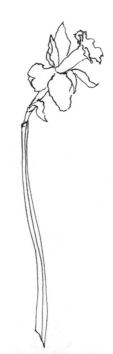

If you meet on the way
a man who knows,
Don't speak a word,
—don't keep silent!

—ZEN SAYING

Layman P'ang

A family man who rejected formal practice but sought enlightenment on his own, Layman P'ang (740–808/811 CE) would inspire countless others through his devotion to the Way. One favorite story tells how Layman freed himself from all possessions by loading them in a boat and sinking it in the middle of a river. Thereupon he and his daughter, Ling-chao, traveled from place to place as itinerant peddlers.

Layman P'ang seems to have known every major Zen figure of his time, studying with them and engaging them in dharma combat. Once, when questioned by Shih-tou about his life, Layman offered the following verse:

> *My daily activities are not unusual,*
> *I'm just naturally in harmony with them.*
> *Grasping nothing, discarding nothing. . . .*
> *Supernatural power and marvelous activity—*
> *Drawing water and carrying firewood.*

He and Ling-chao spent their last two years living in a cave. One day Layman announced that it was time to die and got himself fully prepared, asking his daughter to go outside and report when the sun reached noon. Instead she rushed back in and told him there was an eclipse. When Layman went outside to see it, Ling-chao assumed her father's place and promptly died.

"Her way was always swift," Layman said, and waited a week to follow her.

Zen does not confuse spirituality with thinking about God while one is peeling potatoes. Zen spirituality is just to peel the potatoes.

—ALAN WATTS

Our life is frittered away by detail.... Simplify, simplify.

—HENRY DAVID THOREAU

You are eight years old. It is Sunday evening. You have been granted an extra hour before bed.

The family is playing Monopoly. You have been told that you are big enough to join them.

You lose. You are losing continuously. Your stomach cramps with fear. Nearly all your possessions are gone. The money pile in front of you is almost gone. Your brothers are snatching all the houses from your streets. The last street is being sold. You have to give in. You have lost.

And suddenly you know that it is only a game. You jump up with joy and you knock the big lamp over. It falls on the floor and drags the teapot with it. The others are angry with you, but you laugh when you go upstairs.

You know you are nothing and know you have nothing. And you know that not-to-be and not-to-have give an immeasurable freedom.

—JANWILLEM VAN DE WETERING

Life and love are life and love, a bunch of violets is a bunch of violets, and to drag in the idea of a point is to ruin everything. Live and let live, love and let love, flower and fade, and follow the natural curve, which flows on, pointless.

—D. H. LAWRENCE

A morning-glory
at my window
satisfies me more
than the metaphysics
of books.

—WALT WHITMAN

When Munindra Ji, a vipassana meditation teacher, was asked why he practiced, his response was, "So I will see the tiny purple flowers by the side of the road as I walk to town each day."

With an undefended heart, we can fall in love with life over and over every day. We can become children of wonder, grateful to be walking on earth, grateful to belong with each other and to all of creation. We can find our true refuge in every moment, in every breath. We are happy for no reason.

—TARA BRACH

Lovely snowflakes, they fall nowhere else!

—ZEN SAYING

The crow on the wintry bough, the warbler singing on a windy vine, the bamboo bent with snow, the forever-changing, forever-the-same waterfall or river, the waves that ceaselessly strike the shore—all these were part of the book of life, of that eternal "Isness" at which each man must really look if he hoped to be able to "see."

—NANCY WILSON ROSS

I have a commonplace book for facts, and another for poetry, but I find it difficult always to preserve the vague distinction which I had in mind, for the most interesting and beautiful facts are so much the more poetry and that is their success. They are translated from earth to heaven. I see that if my facts were sufficiently vital and significant— perhaps transmuted into the substance of the human mind—I should need but one book of poetry to contain them all.

—HENRY DAVID THOREAU

When you are deluded and full of doubt, even a thousand books of scripture are not enough.

When you have realized understanding, even one word is too much.

—FEN-YANG

The purpose of a fish trap is to catch
fish, and when the fish are caught,
the trap is forgotten.

The purpose of a rabbit snare is to
catch rabbits. When the rabbits are
caught, the snare is forgotten.

The purpose of words is to convey
ideas. When the ideas are grasped,
the words are forgotten.

Where can I find a man who has
forgotten words? He is the one I would
like to talk to.

—CHUANG TZU

Fletchers bend the arrow; carpenters bend a log of wood; wise people fashion themselves.

—THE BUDDHA

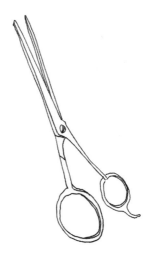

The Buddha

Zen teems with odd answers to the question "What is Buddha?" "Who was the Buddha?" is simpler. Born Siddhartha Guatama in the sixth century BCE in what is today Nepal, the Buddha was a wealthy prince of the Shakya clan. He married, had a son, and lived a pampered life. His father carefully sheltered him from all misery. But during four excursions away from the palace, he encountered four signs—an old man, a sick man, a corpse, and a monk. The first three symbolized humankind's suffering; the fourth, Siddhartha's destiny.

Siddhartha adopted the ascetic homeless path, first with teachers and then, for nine years, on his own. But asceticism proved fruitless. He began to feed his starving body again, and thereby formulate Buddhist ideas about the Middle Path. He then settled under the famed bodhi tree, vowing to meditate until he solved the problem of suffering. Forty-nine days later he achieved his great Enlightenment as the Buddha—and the satori sought after by all Zennists. Reluctant even to speak of it because of its wordless nature, Siddhartha finally addressed a group of disciples, then gave his first discourse in the Deer Park in Benares and spent the rest of his long life teaching. He died at the age of eighty.

Buddha, as he became known, is not the only buddha. According to Buddhist writings, there were six before him and thirteen to follow. The next will be Maitreya, due to come in a future age and renew the dharma.

It is good to have an end to journey toward; but it is the journey that matters, in the end.

—URSULA K. LE GUIN

If a man wishes to be sure of the road he treads on, he must close his eyes and walk in the dark.

—SAINT JOHN OF THE CROSS

Each moment is a place you've never been.

—MARK STRAND

Go—not knowing where.

Bring—not knowing what.

The path is long, the way unknown.

—RUSSIAN FAIRY TALE

The map is not the territory.

—ALFRED KORZYBSKI

The search is what anyone would undertake if he were not sunk in the everydayness of his own life. To become aware of the possibility of the search is to be onto something. Not to be onto something is to be in despair.

—WALKER PERCY

Where do we come from? What are we? Where are we going?

—PAUL GAUGUIN,
INSCRIPTION ON ONE OF HIS PAINTINGS

The journey is my home.

—MURIEL RUKEYSER

In walking, just walk. In sitting, just sit. Above all, don't wobble.

—YUN-MEN

Take one step
away from
yourself—and
behold!—the
Path!

—ABU SA'ID

Living Zen

WALKING

"When you walk, arrive with every step. That is walking meditation. There's nothing else to it."
—Thich Nhat Hanh

In formal Zen practice, periods of *zazen*, or seated meditation, are broken up by shorter periods of *kinhin*, or walking meditation. Practitioners rise after a half hour or so on the cushion and start by taking a very slow, very intentional, stop-breathe-step-repeat walk in a circle around the zendo. At first it feels almost impossible to walk that slowly; our experience conditions us to treat walking as a means to an end rather than the end itself. We walk to get from A to B. We walk for exercise. We walk to clear our heads, or because we have a dog.

But to walk just for the sake of walking is a lovely way to bring mindfulness into your day. Though it need not be as deliberate as the first steps in *kinhin*, try to give it that sense of intention—as an activity or practice to which we give our full attention.

Feel your foot touch the ground. Take a breath. Feel your foot lift, rolling from heel to toe. Feel the second foot follow the first. Breathe again. Feel your body and the pleasure of simply moving. Feel your connection to the ground, to the air, to the world around you, to the moment. It's just you and the earth. Then take another step.

Traveler, there is
no path
The path is made
by walking.

—ANTONIO MACHADO

Our true home is in the
present moment. To live
in the present moment
is a miracle. The miracle
is not to walk on water.
The miracle is to walk
on the green Earth in the
present moment . . .

—THICH NHAT HANH

Zen, which is fundamentally about the emancipation of all beings, is unfortunately sealed in a square box called Zen.

—SŌEN NAKAGAWA

Every exit is an entry somewhere else.

—TOM STOPPARD

One cannot step twice
into the same river.

—HERAKLEITOS

He thought that if he stood on the
bottom rail of a bridge and leant over,
and watched the river slipping slowly
away beneath him, he would suddenly
know everything there was to be known.

—A. A. MILNE

The only joy in the world is to begin.

—CESARE PAVESE

Another time I saw a child coming toward me holding a lighted torch in his hand. "Where have you brought the light from?" I asked him. He immediately blew it out, and said to me, "O Hasan, tell me where it is gone, and I will tell you whence I fetched it."

—HASAN BASRI

A special transmission
  outside the scriptures;
No dependence upon words
  and letters;
Direct pointing to the soul
  of man;
Seeing into one's nature and
  attaining Buddhahood.

—BODHIDHARMA

The Barbarian from the West

"Why did Bodhidharma come from the West?" is a familiar question in Zen literature. The reference is to an Indian Buddhist monk, Bodhidharma (ca. 470–532 BCE), who traveled by boat from India to China during the sixth century BCE and over time became known as the First Patriarch.

The story of Bodhidharma begins with his meeting Emperor Wu, who assailed him with accounts of good Buddhist deeds and asked what merit he gained. "No merit," Bodhidharma replied. "Then what is the first principle of the Holy Teaching?" "Vast emptiness, nothing holy." "Who is confronting me?" the emperor demanded. Bodhidharma said: "I don't know." From there Bodhidharma traveled north and meditated before a wall for nine years. (To keep from falling asleep, one legend has it, he cut off his eyelids; where they fell, tea plants grew, thus crediting him with bringing tea to China.) Before returning to India (or prior to dying in China by poisoning—accounts differ), Bodhidharma installed his student Hui-k'o as the Second Patriarch, and so the lineage began.

Though his teaching remained Indian in character, Bodhidharma is revered as the father of Zen and one who defined its "direct pointing" essence.

A Zen Vocabulary

MUSHIN: no-mind, or detachment of mind; complete freedom from dualistic thinking

SAMADHI: collected concentration in which subject is no different from object

SHIKANTAZA: precisely sitting or meditating, with no supporting techniques, such as counting breaths

MAKYO: a mysterious apparition, particularly a vision or dream arising out of meditation

ZENDO: a meditation hall

Life always gives us
exactly the teacher we need
at every moment.
This includes

> every mosquito, every misfortune,
> every red light,
> every traffic jam, every obnoxious
> supervisor (or employee),
> every illness, every loss, every
> moment of joy or depression,
> every addiction, every piece of
> garbage, every breath.

Every moment is the guru.

—JOAN TOLLIFSON

The true way goes over a rope which is not stretched at any great height but just above the ground. It seems more designed to make people stumble than to be walked upon.

—FRANZ KAFKA

Zen pretty much comes
down to three things—
everything changes;
everything is connected;
pay attention.

—JANE HIRSHFIELD

The Great Way is not difficult for those
　　who have no preferences.
When love and hate are both absent
　　everything becomes clear and
　　undisguised.
Make the smallest distinction however
And heaven and earth are set infinitely
　　apart.

—SENG-TS'AN

Comparisons are odious.

—POPULAR FOURTEENTH-CENTURY SAYING

How shall I grasp it?
Do not grasp it. That which
remains when there is no
more grasping is the Self.

—*PANCHADASI*

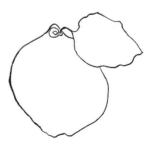

Zen has nothing
to grab on to.
When people who
study Zen don't see
it, that is because
they approach too
eagerly.

—YING-AN

One minute of sitting,
one minute of being
a buddha.

—ZEN SAYING

Don't just do something. Sit there.

—SYLVIA BOORSTEIN

Act without doing; work without effort.

—*TAO TE CHING*

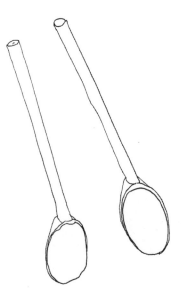

To be a man of knowledge one needs to be light and fluid.

—YAQUI MYSTIC

I take a nap
making the mountain water
pound the rice.

—ISSA

We have forgotten what rocks, plants, and animals still know. We have forgotten how to be.

—ECKHART TOLLE

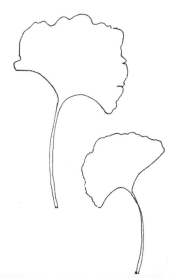

A Zen Vocabulary

DOKUSAN: a private meeting between student and Master in the seclusion of the Master's room; a key element of Rinzai Zen

ROSHI: a venerable teacher, whether a monk or layperson, woman or man

MONDO: a dialogue about Buddhism or an existential problem among Masters or between Master and student

INKA: a seal of enlightenment; a Master's official confirmation that a student has completed training

We think in generalities, but we live in detail.

—ALFRED NORTH WHITEHEAD

Obviously a drawing of a person is not a real person, but a drawing of a line is a real line.

—SOL LEWITT

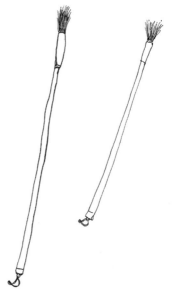

When the student is ready, the Master appears.

—BUDDHIST PROVERB

We don't receive wisdom; we must
discover it for ourselves, after a journey
through the wilderness which no one
else can make for us, which no one can
spare us, for our wisdom is the point
of view from which we come at last to
regard the world.

—MARCEL PROUST

We can be knowledgeable
with other men's knowledge,
but we cannot be wise with
other men's wisdom.

—MICHEL DE MONTAIGNE

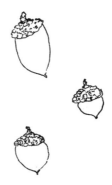

"*Kwatsu!*"

Zen is infamous for the unorthodox methods used by its Masters, particularly those of T'ang Dynasty China who developed Zen's "strange words and extraordinary actions" style of teaching. Yun-men answered his monks' queries with a single word. Ma-tsu knocked students to the ground, twisted their noses, and pioneered the use of the shippei (Japanese, *kyosaku*)—the "wake-up stick" used by meditation monitors.

Lin-chi perfected the "*Ho!*"—a sound that translates in Japanese as *kwatsu*, or just *kwats*, an exclamation used to shock students out of their dualistic thinking. Chao-chou's short, simple, paradoxical statements are unsurpassed for their inventiveness and form the basis of many koans.

And then there was the one-finger Zen of Ch'i-chi. One time an outsider asked Ch'i-chi's attendant what kind of Zen his Master preached. The boy held up just one finger, as did his Master when he was asked a question. On hearing of this, Ch'i-chi cut off the boy's finger with a knife. The boy began to run from the room, screaming with pain. Ch'i-chi called to him. The boy turned around. Ch'i-chi held up one finger. At that the boy was enlightened.

Zen is your everyday thought.

—CHAO-CHOU

If you meet the buddha, kill the buddha.

—LIN-CHI

We're all Buddhas. We just don't recognize it.

—YOUNGEY MINGYUR RINPOCHE

Do not seek to follow in
the footsteps of the wise.
Seek what they sought.

—BASHŌ

Somebody showed it to me and I found it by myself.

—LEW WELCH

No one shows a child the sky.

—AFRICAN PROVERB

Farmer,
pointing the way
with a radish.

—ISSA

You be Bosatsu, I'll be the taxi-driver Driving you home.

—GARY SNYDER

The whole path of mindfulness is this: Whatever you are doing, be aware of it.

—DIPA MA

What is this true meditation? It is to make everything: coughing, swallowing, waving the arms, motion, stillness, words, action, the evil and the good, prosperity and shame, gain and loss, right and wrong, into one single koan.

—HAKUIN

Meditation is not a means to an end. It is both the means and the end.

—KRISHNAMURTI

We don't meditate to get better at meditating, we meditate to get better at life.

—SHARON SALZBERG

that stone Buddha deserves
   all the birdshit it gets
I wave my skinny arms like
   a tall flower in the wind

—IKKYŪ

Water which is too pure has no fish.

—*TS'AI KEN T'AN*

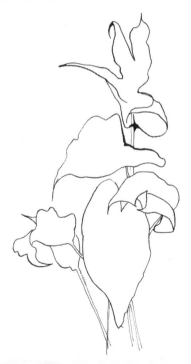

We walk, and our religion is shown
(even to the dullest and most insensitive
person) in how we walk. Or to put it
more accurately, living in this world
means choosing, choosing to walk,
and the way we choose to walk is
infallibly and perfectly expressed in
the walk itself. Nothing can disguise it.
The walk of an ordinary man and of an
enlightened man are as different as that
of a snake and a giraffe.

—R. H. BLYTH

The Sixth Patriarch

One day a poor, uneducated woodcutter named Hui-neng (638–713 CE) overheard monks reciting a line from the Diamond Sutra—"Let your mind flow freely without dwelling on anything." It changed his life and the history of Chinese Zen. Before his death Hui-neng, the Sixth Patriarch, would give Zen a wholly Chinese stamp by merging it with Taoist ideas (e.g., rejection of book learning) and, through his dharma successors, lead Zen into its Golden Age.

The watershed story about this great figure concerns his installment as the Sixth Patriarch. For eight months, Hui-neng had toiled as a kitchen helper in a monastery when its leader, Hung-jen, the Fifth Patriarch, announced it was time to appoint a successor. Hung-jen asked the monks to write a poem expressing their understanding of Zen. The head monk put his verse on a wall:

> *Our body is the bodhi* tree,*
> *And our mind a mirror bright.*
> *Carefully we wipe them hour by hour,*
> *And let no dust alight.*

Hui-neng dictated this version:

> *There is no bodhi tree,*
> *Nor stand of mirror bright.*
> *Since all is void,*
> *Where can the dust alight?*

Hung-jen knew at once who understood his teaching.

---

*The tree under which Buddha sat and attained enlightenment.

However innumerable sentient beings,

I vow to save them all.

However inexhaustible the passions,

I vow to extinguish them all.

However immeasurable the dharmas,

I vow to master them all.

However incomparable the Buddha's

truth, I vow to attain it.

—THE FOUR VOWS

Where there are humans
you'll find flies,
and Buddhas.

—ISSA

The great work of life and death.

—SEUNG SAHN, ON ZEN

For everything that
lives is holy,
life delights in life.

—WILLIAM BLAKE

One day, soon after his enlightenment,
the Buddha was walking toward a man
who, while not knowing who he was,
could see that there was something
different about him. The man came
closer and asked the Buddha:

"Are you a god?"

"No," the Buddha replied.

"Are you a magician, then? A sorcerer?"

"No."

"Are you an angel? Some sort of
celestial being?"

The Buddha again answered, "No."

"What are you then?" the man asked.

The Buddha replied: "I am awake."

—ZEN MONDO

One day the great Master Huang-po and a monk were walking along, talking and laughing together like old friends. When they came to a swollen river, the monk tried to take the Master across, but Huang-po said, "Please cross over yourself."

The monk walked across the waves as though walking on a level field. Once on the other side he called, "Come across! Come across!"

The Master scolded him: "You self-perfected fellow! If I had known you were going to perform a miracle, I would have broken your legs!"

The monk sighed with admiration and said, "You are a true Master of the Great Vehicle."

—ZEN STORY

Unformed people delight in the gaudy and in novelty. Cooked people delight in the ordinary.

—ZEN SAYING

When hungry, eat your rice; when tired, close your eyes. Fools may laugh at me, but wise men will know what I mean.

—LIN-CHI

A Zen Vocabulary

DHARMA: cosmic law, secular law; the teaching of the Buddha; the Way; the general state of affairs; a central concept of Buddhism

KARMA: the Buddhist universal law of cause and effect

NIRVANA: the goal of Buddhism; freedom from karma; extinction of all craving; the realization of the true nature of the mind

TAO: the Way; the source of reality; the truth; the ultimate principle

Those who want the fewest things are nearest to the gods.

—SOCRATES

I threw my cup away
when I saw a child
drinking from his
hands at the trough.

—DIOGENES

Sit

Rest

Work.

Alone with yourself,

Never weary.

On the edge of the forest

Live joyfully,

Without desire.

—THE BUDDHA

This is what you shall do: Love the earth and sun and the animals, despise riches, give alms to everyone that asks, stand up for the stupid and crazy, devote your income and labor to others, hate tyrants, argue not concerning God. . . .

—WALT WHITMAN

When the Many are reduced to One, to what is the One reduced?

—ZEN KOAN

We're all just walking each other home.

—RAM DASS

Do not look for signs.

Do not look for experiences.

Do not be so complicated.

Become like a child.

See everything with awe.

—ROBERT ADAMS

We see men haying far in the meadow,
their heads waving like the grass they
cut. In the distance, the wind seemed to
bend all alike.

—HENRY DAVID THOREAU

Zen and the Art of Haiku

Haiku is the shortest form of poetry known in world literature, but its three little lines of 5-7-5 syllables are capable of expressing deep feeling and sudden flashes of intuition. There is no symbolism in haiku. It catches life as it flows. There is no egotism either; haiku is practically authorless. But in its preoccupation with the simple, seemingly trivial stuff of everyday life—a falling leaf, snow, a fly—haiku shows us how to see into the life of things and gain a glimpse of enlightenment. Haiku is not Zen, but Zen is haiku. It is, in the words of R. H. Blyth, "the final flower of all Eastern culture."

Haiku was elevated to its present form by the great poet Bashō. Other poets include Buson, Issa, Ryōkan, and Shiki. Like all Japanese arts that are bound up with the spirit of Zen, haiku evokes *sabi*, solitude, aloneness or detachment, and *wabi*, the poignant spirit of poverty. Always, a season is mentioned—with plum blossoms for spring, for example, the bare branches for fall. And like all the Zen arts, haiku knows when enough has been said.

The butterfly
Resting upon the
   temple bell,
Asleep.

—BUSON

Look, children, hail-stones! Let's rush out!

—BASHŌ

Today.

—WORD CARVED ON A STONE
ON JOHN RUSKIN'S DESK

Jump.

—JOSEPH CAMPBELL

It was evening all
   afternoon.
It was snowing
And it was going to
   snow.
The blackbird sat
In the cedar-limbs.

—WALLACE STEVENS

If you do not believe,

Look at September!

Look at October!

The yellow leaves falling, falling,

To fill both mountain and river.

—*ZENRIN-KUSHU*

Wisdom is like a clear cool pool—it can
be entered from any side.

Wisdom is like a mass of fire—it cannot
be entered from any side.

—NAGARJUNA

A man walking across a field encountered a tiger. He fled, the tiger chasing after him. Coming to a cliff, he caught hold of a wild vine and swung himself over the edge. The tiger sniffed at him from above. Terrified, the man looked down to where, far below, another tiger had come, waiting to eat him. Two mice, one white and one black, little by little began to gnaw away at the vine. The man saw a luscious strawberry near him. Grasping the vine with one hand, he plucked the strawberry with the other. How sweet it tasted!

—ZEN PARABLE

Barn's burnt down—
now
I can see the moon.

—MASAHIDE

Every day is a good day.

—YUN-MEN

It loved to happen.

—MARCUS AURELIUS

The capacity for
delight is the gift
of paying attention.

—JULIA MARGARET CAMERON

The whole of life lies in the verb *seeing*.

—TEILHARD DE CHARDIN

Living Zen

SEEING

"The meaning of life is to see."
—HUI-NENG

Could it really be that simple? That to understand the meaning of life, we need only open our eyes and look around us?

This kind of mindful seeing means that we hit pause, take a breath, and focus on what's in front of our eyes. That we try to see what we're looking at as if we haven't seen it before, whether it's a flower, an orange, trees on the horizon, or the view from our desk. An easy metaphor to reach for is to see as if through the eyes of a child, where everything is infused with wonder.

To see an orange for the first time—with wonder— start here: Pick one up and look—really look—without any expectation. Look at the texture, the color, the shape, all the little nubs on the rind, the different shades. Hold it up to a window, or under a lamp. Think of it like meditation, where you let go of distractions (the little left-brained voice inside yammering, *It's just an orange, you've seen a million of them, why are you wasting precious time?!*) and understand that this orange, like this moment, is unique.

Try the same thing with other objects, or even people. Look at a pencil. The keys to your home. The face of your child or partner or pet. It's important that our brains glide over these everyday things—it would be exhausting, otherwise, to see everything as if you'd never seen it before. (*Is it edible? Do I know this person? What do I do with this round piece of shiny metal?*) But to only glide over is just another way where we don't really participate in our own lives—exactly what mindfulness helps counter.

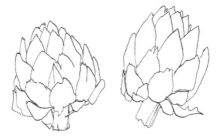

When the eye wakes up to see again, it suddenly stops taking anything for granted.

—FREDERICK FRANCK

The moment one gives close attention to anything, even a blade of grass, it becomes a mysterious, awesome, indescribably magnificent world in itself.

—HENRY MILLER

It's called enlightenment.
It's nothing more or less
than seeing things as they
are rather than as we wish
or believe them to be.

—STEVEN HAGEN

It is only with the heart that one can see rightly; what is essential is invisible to the eye.

—ANTOINE DE SAINT-EXUPÉRY

In dwelling, live close to the ground.

In thinking, keep to the simple.

In conflict, be fair and generous.

In governing, don't try to control.

In work, do what you enjoy.

In family life, be completely present.

—*TAO TE CHING*

Once at Cold Mountain, troubles

cease—

No more tangled, hung-up mind.

I idly scribble poems on the rock cliff,

Taking whatever comes, like a drifting

boat.

—HAN SHAN

Catch the vigorous horse of your mind.

—ZEN SAYING

Let the nothingness into yer shots.

—MICHAEL MURPHY, *GOLF IN THE KINGDOM*

When someone tosses you

a tea bowl

—Catch it!

Catch it nimbly with soft

cotton.

With the cotton of your

skillful mind!

—BANKEI

I hear the wind blow,
and I feel that
it was worth being
born just to
hear the wind blow.

—FERNANDO PESSOA

How much better is silence; the coffee cup, the table. How much better to sit by myself like the solitary sea-bird that opens its wings on the stake. Let me sit here forever with bare things, this coffee cup, this knife, this fork, things in themselves, myself being myself.

—VIRGINIA WOOLF

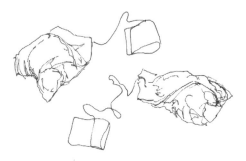

Zen and the Art of Tea

Since the time of Bodhidharma, tea and Zen have been connected. Fittingly, it was one of Japan's first Zen Masters, Eisai, who brought tea seeds from China. And it was the Zen student Rikyu who refined the art of tea, *cha-no-yu*, in the sixteenth century.

Like Zen, the art of tea aims at simplification. It consists simply of boiling water, preparing tea, and drinking it. Its spirit conjures up harmony, reverence, purity, tranquility, poverty, solitariness; and it has deeply influenced the arts of flower arranging, pottery, and architecture. The ceremony itself is practiced in a simple thatched hut—the "abode of vacancy." The utensils are few and unpretentious, and there is nothing else in the room except perhaps an arrangement of flowers or a single painting.

No more than four or five guests can be in the tea room, and they are welcomed by the singing of the kettle—pieces of iron are arranged inside it to create sounds that suggest a far-off waterfall or wind blowing through pines. An elaborate set of rules dictate how the thick green tea is whisked and served, how utensils should be passed and admired—all, paradoxically, to achieve tea's state of artless art.

To be fully alive, fully human, and completely awake is to be continually thrown out of the nest. To live fully is to be always in no-man's-land, to experience each moment as completely new and fresh. To live is to be willing to die over and over again.

—PEMA CHÖDRÖN

Our Father which art in heaven

Stay there

And we will stay on earth

Which is sometimes so pretty.

—JACQUES PRÉVERT

We consider bibles and religions
    divine—
I do not say they are not divine,
I say they have all grown out of you, and
may grow out of you still,
It is not they who give the life, it is you
who give the life,
Leaves are no more shed from the trees,
or trees from the earth, than they are
shed out of you.

—WALT WHITMAN

God is so omnipresent . . . God is an angel in an angel, and a stone in a stone, and a straw in a straw.

—JOHN DONNE

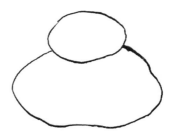

A hand-rolled
Dumpling of
Heaven-and-earth:
I've gulped it down
And easily it went.

—ZEN SAYING

The squeaking of
the pump sounds as
necessary as the music
of the spheres.

—HENRY DAVID THOREAU

The Red Wheelbarrow

so much depends

upon

a red wheel

barrow

glazed with rain

water

beside the white

chickens

—WILLIAM CARLOS WILLIAMS

Do not, I beg you, look for anything behind phenomena. They are themselves their own lesson.

—JOHANN WOLFGANG VON GOETHE

It is only shallow people who do not judge by appearances.

—OSCAR WILDE

At the moment you are most in awe of all there is about life that you don't understand, you are closer to understanding it all than at any other time.

—JANE WAGNER

A Zen Vocabulary

PRAJNA: intuitive wisdom, insight into emptiness or the true nature of reality

SHUNYATA: emptiness or void, without essence; a key notion of Buddhism

HARA: belly or gut, which is a person's spiritual center

SAMSARA: succession of rebirths

HINAYANA: literally "Small Vehicle," the Northern Buddhist term for the Southern Buddhism of Southeast Asia

MAHAYANA: "Great Vehicle," the Northern Buddhism of China, Korea, and Japan

God made everything out of nothing. But the nothingness shows through.

—PAUL VALÉRY

Picture a massless particle.

—A KOAN OF MODERN PHYSICS

We shape clay into a pot,

but it is the emptiness inside

that holds whatever we want.

—*TAO TE CHING*

The notes I handle
no better than many
pianists. But the
pauses between the
notes—ah, that is
where the art resides!

—ARTHUR SCHNABEL

I have never
waited for
anything the
way I've waited
for today, when
nothing will
happen.

—MARGUERITE DURAS

Even a good thing isn't as good as nothing.

—ZEN SAYING

Among the great things which are to be found among us, the Being of Nothingness is the greatest.

—LEONARDO DA VINCI

I have nothing to say, I am saying it, and that is poetry.

—JOHN CAGE

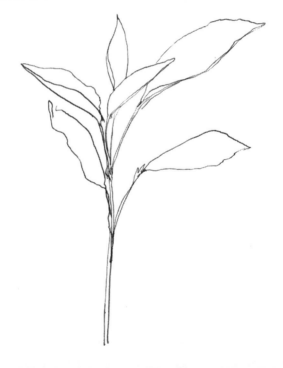

You say my poems
   are poetry?
They are not.
Yet if you understand
   they are not—
Then you see the
   poetry of them.

—RYŌKAN

No one's mouth is big enough to utter the whole thing.

—ALAN WATTS

Say one word with your mouth shut!

—ZEN SAYING

Enlightenment

Awakening—*satori*, or *kensho*—is the fundamental aim of Zen. It is seeing into your nature, realizing your own Buddhahood, freeing yourself from the cycle of birth and death. It is "to die completely and then come back to life." According to the koan text *Denkoroku*, "Even if you sit until your seat breaks through . . . even if you are a person of lofty deeds and pure behavior, if you haven't reached *satori* you can't get out of the prison of the world."

Zen writing is filled with examples of unexpected things that trigger enlightenment: Buddha seeing the morning star, Bankei coughing up a blood clot, Hsiang-yen hearing a pebble strike a bamboo tree. But one of the best descriptions of the actual experience comes from the Master Sokei-an Sasaki:

"One day I wiped out all notions from my mind. I gave up all desire. I discarded all the words with which I thought and stayed in quietude. I felt a little queer—as if I were being carried into something, or as if I were touching some power unknown to me . . . and Ztt! I entered. I lost the boundary of my physical body. I had my skin, of course, but I felt I was standing in the center of the cosmos. I spoke, but my words had lost their meaning. I saw people coming toward me, but all were the same man. All were myself! I had never known this world. I had believed that I was created, but now I must change my opinion: I was never created; I was the cosmos; no individual Mr. Sasaki existed."

Enlightenment is like the moon reflected on the water. The moon does not get wet, nor is the water broken. Although its light is wide and great, the moon is reflected even in a puddle an inch wide. The whole moon and the entire sky are reflected in one dewdrop on the grass.

—DŌGEN

Let me give you a wonderful Zen practice. Wake up in the morning... look in the mirror, and laugh at yourself.

—BERNIE GLASSMAN

Every day Zuigan called to himself: "Master!"

And every day he answered: "Yes, sir!"

"Become sober," he said.

"Yes, sir!" he answered.

"And do not be deceived by others," he added next.

"Yes, sir, yes sir!" Zuigan answered himself.

—ZEN MONDO

The basic lesson of Zen is, "Forget yourself."

—ROBERT AITKEN

A good practice is to ask yourself very sincerely, "Why was I born?" Ask yourself this question three times a day, in the morning, in the afternoon, and at night. Ask every day.

—AJAHN CHAH

The great path has no gates,

Thousands of roads enter it.

When one passes through this

gateless gate,

He walks freely between heaven and

earth.

—*MUMONKAN*

The bottom of a pail, broken through.

—A ZEN MASTER, ON ENLIGHTENMENT

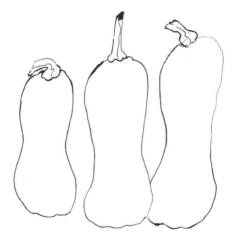

Even if our efforts of attention seem for years to be producing no result, one day a light that is in exact proportion to them will flood the soul.

—SIMONE WEIL

Ten years' searching in
the deep forest
Today great laughter at
the edge of the lake.

—SŌEN

To study Buddhism is to study the self. To study the self is to forget the self. To forget the self is to be enlightened by all things. To be enlightened by all things is to drop off our own body and mind, and to drop off the bodies and minds of others. No trace of enlightenment remains, and this no-trace continues endlessly.

—DŌGEN

Anything more than the truth would be too much.

—ROBERT FROST

At night, deep in the mountains,

I sit in meditation.

The affairs of men never reach here:

Everything is quiet and empty,

All the incense has been swallowed up

by the endless night.

My robe has become a garment of dew.

Unable to sleep I walk out into the

woods—

Suddenly, above the highest peak,

the full moon appears.

—RYŌKAN

Every time
I close the
door on reality
it comes in
through the
window.

—JENNIFER YANE

Crazy Cloud

An eccentric genius revered as much for his wit as for his understanding, Ikkyū Sojun (1394–1481) is a beloved figure in Japanese Zen. He was rumored to be the son of an emperor and lady-in-waiting. A brilliant child, he delighted in exposing the hypocrisy of the stultified and corrupt Zen of his era. Later, he sought out the most uncompromising teacher of his day. After years of pushing himself through severe training, he experienced a sudden enlightenment when, drifting in a boat across Lake Biwa at night, a crow raucously cawed.

After the death of his Master, Ikkyū wandered for the next thirty years, living among all segments of society—nobles, merchants, prostitutes, authors, and artists. He enjoyed the pleasures of women and sake, and continued to spit in the face of orthodoxy.

Ikkyū, who gave himself the name "Crazy Cloud," was an influential painter, calligrapher, and poet. On the opposite page are two of his most beloved poems.

Void In Form

When, just as they are,

White dewdrops gather

On scarlet maple leaves,

Regard the scarlet beads!

Form In Void

The tree is stripped,

All color, fragrance gone,

Yet already on the bough,

Uncaring spring!

Consider the lilies of the field, how they grow; they toil not, neither do they spin:

And yet I say unto you, That even Solomon in all his glory was not arrayed like one of these.

—MATTHEW 6:28–29

When it blows,
The mountain wind is
boisterous,
But when it blows not,
It simply blows not.

—EMILY BRONTË

Late on the third day, at the very
moment when, at sunset, we were
making our way through a herd of
hippopotamuses, there flashed upon
my mind, unforeseen and unsought,
the phrase, "Reverence for Life."

—ALBERT SCHWEITZER

The rocks are where they are—
this is their will. The rivers
flow—this is their will. The
birds fly—this is their will.
Human beings talk—this is
their will. The seasons change,
heaven sends down rain or
snow, the earth occasionally
shakes, the waves roll, the stars
shine—each of them follows its
own will. To be is to will and so
is to become.

—D. T. SUZUKI

What's this little brown insect

   walking zigzag

across the sunny white page of

   Su Tung-p'o's poem?

Fly away, tiny mite, even your life

   is tender—

I lift the book and blow you into

   the dazzling void.

—ALLEN GINSBERG

Don't kill him!
    the fly it wrings its hands,
        its feet.

—ISSA

A branch shorn of leaves
a crow perching on it—
this autumn eve.

—BASHŌ

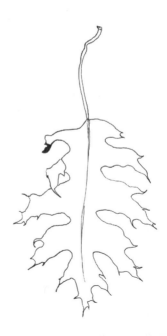

IN A STATION OF THE METRO

The apparition of these faces in the
  crowd;
Petals on a wet, black bough.

—EZRA POUND

this ink painting of wind

blowing through pines:

who hears it?

—IKKYŪ

The wind blows hard
among the pines ...
Listen: you've heard
everything.

—SHINKICHI TAKAHASHI

Sitting quietly,
doing nothing,
spring comes,
and the grass
grows by itself.

—ZEN SAYING

Of course the Dharma-body of the Buddha was the hedge at the bottom of the garden. At the same time, no less obviously, it was these flowers, it was anything that I—or rather the blessed Not-I—cared to look at.

—ALDOUS HUXLEY

To see a World in a Grain of Sand,

And a Heaven in a Wild Flower,

Hold infinity in the palm of your hand,

And eternity in an hour.

—WILLIAM BLAKE

To make a prairie it takes a clover

    and one bee,

One clover, and a bee.

And revery.

The revery alone will do,

If bees are few.

—EMILY DICKINSON

Bashō

Though not a Zen monk, Matsuo Bashō (1644–1694), Japan's greatest poet and one of the great lyric poets in any language, elevated the haiku form to the level of art and infused it with the spirit of Zen and the Tao. "Learn the rules well, and then forget them," he advised his students. He also told them: "Go to the pine if you want to learn about the pine, or to the bamboo if you want to learn about the bamboo. And in so doing you must let go of your subjective preoccupation with yourself. . . . Your poetry arises by itself when you and the object have become one."

Bashō revered nature, children, the moon. He found the universe in the smallest detail, which he saw with the innocent eye of a child, and spent his later years on often lonely pilgrimages across Japan. "Old Pond," his best-known haiku, has been interpreted as a kind of koan, the frog disclosing the final meaning of reality:

> *Old pond,*
> *frog jumps in—*
> *plop.*

The melons look cool
flecked with mud
from the morning dew.

—BASHŌ

We gaze
even at horses
this morn of snow.

—BASHŌ

Each portion of matter may be conceived of as a garden full of plants, and as a pond full of fishes. But each branch of the plant, each member of the animal, each drop of its humors, is also such a garden or such a pond.

—GOTTFRIED LEIBNIZ

Spend the afternoon. You can't take it with you.

—ANNIE DILLARD

Butter tea and wind
pictures, the Crystal
Mountain, and blue sheep
dancing on the snow—
it's quite enough!

Have you seen the snow
leopard?

No! Isn't that wonderful?

—PETER MATTHIESSEN

Moonlight through
high branches,
Is being nothing else
But moonlight
through high
branches.

—FERNANDO PESSOA

All journeys have secret destinations of which the traveler is unaware.

—MARTIN BUBER

Goodnight stars.
Goodnight air.

—MARGARET WISE BROWN

A heavy snowfall disappears into the sea. What silence!

—ZEN SAYING

Knock on the sky and listen to the sound!

—ZEN SAYING

This magnificent butterfly finds a little heap of dirt and sits still on it; but man will never on his heap of mud keep still.

—JOSEPH CONRAD

With the evening breeze

the water laps

against the heron's legs.

—BUSON

One real world is enough.

—GEORGE SANTAYANA

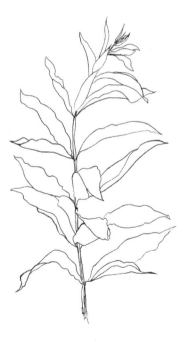

Be present in all things and thankful for all things.

—MAYA ANGELOU

A page from a journal of modern experimental physics will be as mysterious to the uninitiated as a Tibetan mandala. Both are records of enquiries into the nature of the universe.

—FRITJOF CAPRA

Modern Physics

Found in the beginning of the Heart Sutra, a Buddhist work that holds a preeminent place in Zen, are the words:

Form is no different from emptiness.
Emptiness is no different from form.
Form is precisely emptiness,
emptiness is precisely form.

Two thousand years later, Western physicists agree.

Science's concept of the universe was changed irrevocably by quantum mechanics and Einstein's theory of relativity, which questioned the separate identity of energy and matter. Our comfortable ideas of a universe made up of solid little bits of matter behaving in logical ways have been exploded. A particle is not a separate entity but a set of relationships. The world is an interconnected tissue of events, a dynamic unbroken whole. Scientists are no longer observers but participants. And physics and mysticism converge in striking parallels, leading back full circle. Or, as Gary Zukav put it in *The Dancing Wu Li Masters*:

"A powerful awareness lies dormant in these discoveries [of modern physics]: an awareness of the hitherto-unsuspected powers of the mind to mold 'reality', rather than the other way around. In this sense the philosophy of physics is becoming indistinguishable from the philosophy of Buddhism, which is the philosophy of enlightenment."

Perhaps ultimately, spiritual simply means experiencing wholeness and interconnectedness directly, a seeing that individuality and the totality are interwoven, that nothing is separate or extraneous. If you see in this way, then everything becomes spiritual in its deepest sense. Doing science is spiritual. So is washing the dishes. It is the inner experience which counts. And you have to be there for it. All else is mere thinking.

—JON KABAT-ZINN

Nothing is absolute.
Everything changes,
everything moves,
everything revolves,
everything flies and
goes away.

—FRIDA KAHLO

It's always *just* beginning.
Everything is always *just*
beginning.

—JAKUSHO KWONG

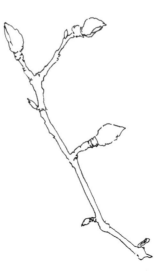

Don't be afraid to be confused. Try to remain permanently confused.

—GEORGE SAUNDERS

Don't try to understand! It's enough if you do not misunderstand.

—NISARGADATTA MAHARAJ

Living Zen

BREATHING

"In this very breath that we take now lies the secret that all great teachers try to tell us."
—Peter Matthiessen

The essence of mindfulness is to stay present and pay attention to what is happening here and now. It sounds so simple, yet it is anything but. We live in a world that feels intentionally designed to distract us, and it comes at us from all sides—the phone in our hands, the traffic swirling on our streets, ads, TV, online shopping, all the social media. Multitasking is now our baseline.

But to paraphrase Peter Matthiessen, we all hold the great secret that can quiet this distraction, restore our attention, and return us to the present: the breath.

The moment we pay attention to our breath, everything changes. Try it. Stop, sit up, and just focus on your breathing, an in-breath followed by an out-breath, an in-breath followed by an out-breath. Notice how noise

drops away, how the mind grows still, how we become
aware again of our body. Notice the feeling of a greater
awareness, and also a sense of being re-centered, of
finding a calm point in the heart of a storm.

Try it at your desk, when you need to focus. Try it
when you're feeling anxious. Try it just before you're about
to walk into a room full of strangers. Or try it every day at
3:00, just to reconnect.

Is it enlightenment? Perhaps not. But it is a moment
reclaimed, a moment of peace and presence. And just
imagine—this profound gift, the wisdom of the breath, is
available whenever we need it. Our life started with the
breath and it is the surest way to return to the pure
awareness of being alive.

If we ask, for instance, whether the position of the electron remains the same, we must say "no"; if we ask whether the electron's position changes with time, we must say "no"; if we ask whether the electron is at rest, we must say "no"; if we ask whether it is in motion, we must say "no."

—J. ROBERT OPPENHEIMER

Enlightened people can still remember their phone numbers.

—GARY ZUKAV

The "silly question"
is the first intimation
of some totally new
development.

—ALFRED NORTH WHITEHEAD

The world is charged with the grandeur of God.

—GERARD MANLEY HOPKINS

The Buddha, the Godhead, resides
quite as comfortably in the circuits of a
digital computer or the gears of a cycle
transmission as he does at the top of a
mountain or in the petals of a flower.
To think otherwise is to demean the
Buddha—which is to demean oneself.

—ROBERT M. PIRSIG

The practice of Zen is not limited to the meditation mat. The practice of Zen is our entire life and is the very thread that binds our different lives together. Discovering this truth is called awakening, and it can take a circuitous route.

—JANET JIRYU ABELS

To ask the hard question is simple.

—W. H. AUDEN

What is your original face before your mother and father were born?

—ZEN KOAN

It is as hard to see one's self as to look backwards without turning around.

—HENRY DAVID THOREAU

Search back into your own vision—think back to the mind that thinks. Who is it?

—WU-MEN

The trouble is, you think you have time . . .

—JACK KORNFIELD

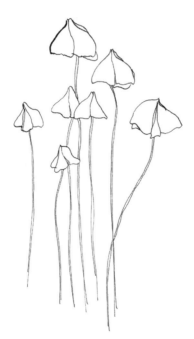

A monk brought two potted plants to his Master.

"Drop it," ordered the Master.

The monk dropped one pot.

"Drop it," again ordered the Master.

The monk let the second pot go.

"Drop it," now roared the Master.

The monk stammered: "But I have nothing to drop."

The Master nodded. "Then take it away."

—ZEN MONDO

Get rid of the self and act from the Self!

—ZEN SAYING

The true value of a human being can be found in the degree to which he has attained liberation from the self.

—ALBERT EINSTEIN

Zen in its essence is the art of seeing into the nature of one's being, and it points the way from bondage to freedom.

—D. T. SUZUKI

D. T. Suzuki

In a historic feat of cultural transmission, the lay Zen student and scholar Daisetz Teitaro Suzuki (1870–1966) introduced generations of Westerners to Zen Buddhism. Beginning with a translation of *Ashvagosha's Discourse on the Awakening of Faith in the Mahayana*, D. T. Suzuki published dozens of books and articles that clarified Zen for Westerners. Avoiding both historical and philosophical analysis, he presented Zen as "a wafting cloud in the sky. No screw fastens it, no string holds it. . . ."

By the 1950s, when he settled in New York and taught classes at Columbia to the likes of Erich Fromm, John Cage, Karen Horney, and others, Suzuki had caught the popular imagination. His books, direct, humorous, grounded in experience and scholarship, were turning up in paperback. He was profiled in *The New Yorker* and interviewed on television. In Thomas Merton's words, "In meeting him one seemed to meet that 'True Man of No Title' that the Zen Masters speak of. And of course this is the man one really wants to meet."

"Zen is the ultimate fact of all philosophy," wrote Suzuki. "That final psychic fact that takes place when religious consciousness is heightened to extremity . . . in Buddhists, in Christians, in philosophers."

Whatever is happening is the path to enlightenment.

—PEMA CHÖDRÖN

The purpose of Zen is the perfection of character.

—YAMADA ROSHI

One day Chao-chou fell down in the snow, and called out, "Help me up! Help me up!" A monk came and lay down beside him. Chao-chou got up and went away.

—ZEN KOAN

The more we understand individual things, the more we understand God.

—BARUCH SPINOZA

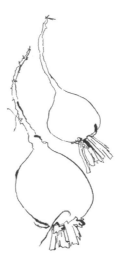

If you gaze for long into the abyss, the abyss also gazes into you.

—FRIEDRICH NIETZSCHE

The most terrifying thing is to accept oneself completely.

—CARL JUNG

Who *is* the Potter, pray, and who the Pot?

—THE RUBÁIYÁT OF OMAR KHAYYÁM

He who knows others
is wise.
He who knows himself
is enlightened.

—*TAO TE CHING*

Everything you know is wrong.

—THE FIRESIGN THEATRE

Your problem is how you are going to spend this one odd and precious life you have been issued. Whether you're going to spend it trying to look good and creating the illusion that you have power over people and circumstances, or whether you are going to taste it, enjoy it, and find out the truth about who you are.

—ANNE LAMOTT

A Great Fool

Daigu Ryōkan (literally "Great Fool") is one of the most beloved figures in Japanese folk tradition. A Zen poet-monk, he loved children and playing a happy game of ball, which he called "the highest form of Zen."

After receiving the seal of enlightenment from his Soto Master, Ryōkan (1758–1831) chose not to take students but to emulate the monks of old, living in solitude as a mountain hermit and relying on alms for sustenance. He endured bitter periods of poverty, yet never lost his extraordinary innocence and loving heart. When a burglar ransacked his hut after discovering nothing of value, Ryōkan wrote a haiku:

> *The thief left it there*
> > *there in the window—*
> > > *the shining moon.*

Ryōkan wrote poetry that is among the most beautiful in Zen literature. But he also left behind his "Great Fool's" essence, as in the popular story about a game of hide-and-seek. As it grew dark, the children seeking Ryōkan went home, but the monk continued hiding. The next morning a farmer found Ryōkan behind a haystack. "Hush," he said, "or the children will find me!"

I am a writer who came from a sheltered life. A sheltered life can be a daring life as well. For all serious daring starts from within.

—EUDORA WELTY

Can you walk on water? You have done no better than a straw. Can you fly in the air? You have done no better than a bluebottle. Conquer your heart; then you may become somebody.

—ANSARI OF HERAT

We can always begin again.

—SHARON SALZBERG

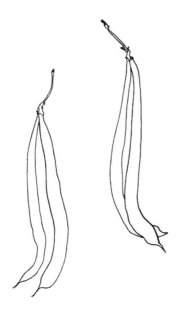

How could there be any question of acquiring or possessing, when the one thing needful for a man is to become— to be at last, and to die in the fullness of his being.

—ANTOINE DE SAINT-EXUPÉRY

The self says, I am;

The heart says, I am
   less;

The spirit says, you are
   nothing.

—THEODORE ROETHKE

If you let go a little

You will have a little happiness. If you let

go a lot

You will have a lot of happiness. If you

let go completely

You will be free.

—AJAHN CHAH

That which transcends both the self and the other, that's what my teaching is about. Let me prove this to you: While everyone is turned this way to hear me, out back there may be sparrows chirping, human voices calling, or the sighing of the wind. But, without your consciously trying to hear them, each of those sounds comes to you clearly recognized and distinguished. It's not you doing the hearing, so it's not a matter of the self. But since no one else does your hearing for you, you couldn't call it the other! When you listen this way with the Unborn Buddha-mind you transcend whatever there is.

—BANKEI

See without looking,
hear without listening,
breathe without asking.

—W. H. AUDEN

Reality only reveals itself
when it is illuminated by
a ray of poetry.

—GEORGES BRAQUE

Sometimes I go about in pity for myself,
and all the while
A great wind is bearing me across the
sky.

—OJIBWA SAYING

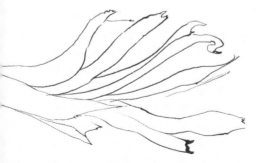

The aim of life is to live, and to live means to be aware, joyously, drunkenly, serenely, divinely aware.

—HENRY MILLER

Be in love with your life. Every minute of it.

—JACK KEROUAC

The living moment is everything.

—D. H. LAWRENCE

Later, he remembered certain moments
in which the power of this moment was
already contained, as in a seed. He thought
of the hour in that other southern garden
(Capri) when the call of a bird did not, so
to speak, break off at the edge of his body,
but was simultaneously outside and in his
innermost being, uniting both into one
uninterrupted space in which, mysteriously
protected, only one single place of purest,
deepest consciousness remained. On that
occasion he had closed his eyes . . . and the
Infinite passed into him from all sides, so
intimately that he believed he could feel the
stars which had in the meantime appeared,
gently reposing within his breast.

—RAINER MARIA RILKE

Thus shall ye think of all this fleeting
    world:
A star at dawn, a bubble in a stream;
A flash of lightning in a summer cloud,
A flickering lamp, a phantom, and a
    dream.

—THE BUDDHA

When I dance, I dance; when I
sleep, I sleep; yes, and when I walk
alone in a beautiful orchard, if my
thoughts drift to far-off matters
for some part of the time, for some
other part I lead them back again
to the walk, the orchard, to the
sweetness of this solitude, to myself.

—MICHEL DE MONTAIGNE

Right now a moment of time is fleeting by! Capture its reality in paint! To do that we must put all else out of our minds. We must become that moment, make ourselves a sensitive recording plate . . . give the image of what we actually see, forgetting everything that has been seen before our time.

—PAUL CÉZANNE

It is a bit embarrassing to have been concerned with the human problem all one's life and find at the end that one has no more to offer by way of advice than "try to be a little kinder."

—ALDOUS HUXLEY

Death Poetry

Traditionally, a Zen Master would write a poem when he was about to die. Charged with his spirit, the Master's poem served both as a summation of life and as a parting gift to inspire his disciples.

Some chastise gently:

> *Coming and going, life and death:*
> *A thousand hamlets, a million houses.*
> *Don't you get the point?*
> *Moon in the water, blossom in the sky.*
>
> —GIZAN

Some say a relieved good-bye after a hard life:

> *Finally out of reach—*
> *No bondage, no dependency.*
> *How calm the ocean,*
> *Towering the void.*
>
> —TESSHO

Some merely shrug:

> *Life as we*
> *Find it—death too.*
> *A parting poem?*
> *Why insist?*
>
> —TA-HUI TSUNG-KAO

And some exult:

> *Four and fifty years*
> *I've hung the sky with stars.*
> *Now I leap through—*
> *What shattering!*
>
> —DŌGEN

Let me respectfully remind you,

Life and death are of supreme

   importance.

Time swiftly passes by and opportunity

   is lost.

Each of us should strive to awaken . . .

awaken . . . Take heed.

Do not squander your life.

—*THE EVENING GATHA*

Oh, one world at a time.

—HENRY DAVID THOREAU,
WHEN ASKED ABOUT THE HEREAFTER

Get up and do
something useful,
the work is part
of the koan!

—HAKUIN

Chop wood, carry water.

—ZEN SAYING

Lift the stone and you will find me; cleave the wood and I am there.

—JESUS, GOSPEL OF THOMAS 77:2–3

A monk asked Chao-chou, "I have just entered the monastery: please give me some guidance."

Chao-chou said, "Have you eaten your rice gruel?"

The monk said, "Yes, I've eaten."

Chao-chou said, "Then go wash your bowl."

—ZEN MONDO

Dōgen

While Zen was still in its infancy in Japan, a gifted monk named Dōgen (1200–1253) made the hazardous voyage to China to seek the Way. Although he would meet many Masters and receive a certificate of enlightenment, it was perhaps the old Chinese monastery cook, visiting the newly landed ship to buy Japanese mushrooms, who gave Dōgen his purest taste of Zen. Dōgen asked the cook to stay and talk, but he begged off, saying he must get back to his duties. When the surprised Dōgen asked him why he didn't practice *zazen* and leave the food to others, the old cook scoffed. Did the ignorant Japanese monk know nothing of the spirit of Buddhism?

Dōgen, who would go on to become not only the most important Soto Zen Master in Japan but also one of humankind's great religious spirits, never forgot the lessons of the cook—that work is fundamentally important to Zen and that enlightenment can be found in even the most ordinary places and acts. "Each and every extraordinary activity," he wrote, "is simply having rice."

When a fish swims, it swims on and on, and there is no end to the water. When a bird flies, it flies on and on, and there is no end to the sky. There was never a fish that swam out of the water, or a bird that flew out of the sky. When they need a little water or sky, they use just a little; when they need a lot, they use a lot. Thus they use all of it at every moment, and in every place they have perfect freedom.

—DŌGEN

There is no end to the opening up that is possible for a human being.

—CHARLOTTE JOKO BECK

1. Out of clutter, find simplicity.

2. From discord, find harmony.

3. In the middle of difficulty lies opportunity.

—ALBERT EINSTEIN, THREE RULES OF WORK

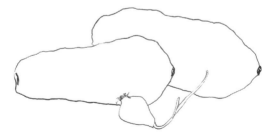

Work is love made visible.
And if you cannot work
with love but only with
distaste, it is better that you
should leave your work and
sit at the gate of the temple
and take alms of those who
work with joy.

—KAHLIL GIBRAN

So the thing to do when working on a motorcycle, as in any other task, is to cultivate the peace of mind which does not separate one's self from one's surroundings. When that is done successfully, then everything else follows naturally. Peace of mind produces right values, right values produce right thoughts. Right thoughts produce right actions and right actions produce work which will be a material reflection for others to see of the serenity at the center of it all.

—ROBERT M. PIRSIG

He did each single thing as if he did nothing else.

—CHARLES DICKENS

That is happiness: to be dissolved into something complete and great.

—WILLA CATHER

Draw bamboos for ten years, become a bamboo, then forget all about bamboos when you are drawing.

—GEORGES DUTHUIT, ON PAINTING IN CHINA

Zen and the Art of Painting and Calligraphy

One of the most highly regarded art forms in East Asia, calligraphy is considerably older than Zen, and not all outstanding examples are Zen-related. But from its beginnings Zen found a natural affinity with the demanding, spontaneous quality of the ink brush. Using the heightened powers of concentration gained by meditation, Zen practitioners were capable of the most creative expression in calligraphy. As the Chinese Zen poet Huang T'ing-chien noticed, calligraphy changed after attaining enlightenment, the clear, sharp lines possessed of a new inner vitality.

Ink painting is Zen art at its highest expression. Zen painters demonstrate a profound communion with nature. The painter approaches his canvas as part of his practice, as contemplation, "empty canvas, blank mind." Beauty is a secondary consideration, with asymmetry, rather than balance, the aim. And empty space is as real as objects and solids; what is left out is as important as what is left in. Using a loaded ink brush on white silk or rice paper requires the utmost control. The first stroke is the final stroke; there can be no subsequent correction. Full of silence, timelessness, and transparency, the paintings hint at an absolute reality beyond which nothing can be said. They are, in the words of one Western art historian, "ciphers of transcendence."

A monk asked Ts'ui-wei about the meaning of Buddhism. Ts'ui-wei answered: "Wait until there is no one around, and I will tell you." Some time later the monk approached Ts'ui-wei again, saying: "There is nobody here now. Please answer me." Ts'ui-wei led him out into the garden and went over to the bamboo grove, saying nothing. Still the monk did not understand, so at last Ts'ui-wei said: "Here is a tall bamboo; there is a short one!"

—ZEN PARABLE

Life is denied by lack of attention, whether it be to cleaning windows or trying to write a masterpiece.

—NADIA BOULANGER

How can you think and hit at the same time?

—YOGI BERRA

The prayer of the monk is not perfect
until he no longer recognizes himself or
the fact that he is praying.

—SAINT ANTHONY

I believe a blade of grass is no less than the journey-work of the stars.

—WALT WHITMAN

If you study Japanese art, you see a man who is undoubtedly wise, philosophic, and intelligent, who spends his time how? In studying the distance between the earth and the moon? No. In studying the policy of Bismarck? No. He studies a single blade of grass. But this blade of grass leads him to draw every plant and then the seasons, then wide aspects of the countryside, then animals, then the human figure. So he passes his life, and life is too short to do the whole.

—VINCENT VAN GOGH

—Children, one earthly Thing truly experienced, even once, is enough for a lifetime.

—RAINER MARIA RILKE

When you understand one thing through and through, you understand everything.

—SHUNRYŪ SUZUKI

What is the color of wind?

—ZEN KOAN

Don't look for miracles. You
yourself are the miracle.

—HENRY MILLER

The world is its own magic.

—SHUNRYŪ SUZUKI

Isn't it enough to see that a garden is beautiful without having to believe that there are fairies at the bottom of it too?

—DOUGLAS ADAMS

The mystical is not how the world is, but that it is.

—LUDWIG WITTGENSTEIN

No ideas but in things.

—WILLIAM CARLOS WILLIAMS

After we came out of the church, we
stood talking for some time together of
Bishop Berkeley's ingenious sophistry
to prove the non-existence of matter,
and that everything in the universe is
merely ideal. I observed that though
we are satisfied his doctrine is not true,
it is impossible to refute it. I shall never
forget the alacrity with which [Samuel]
Johnson answered, striking his foot with
mighty force against a large stone . . .
"I refute it thus!"

—WESTERN MONDO

Fa-yen, a Chinese Zen teacher, overheard four monks arguing about subjectivity and objectivity. He joined them and said: "There is a big stone. Do you consider it to be inside or outside your mind?"

One of the monks replied: "From the Buddhist viewpoint everything is an objectification of mind, so I would say that the stone is inside my mind."

"Your head must feel very heavy," observed Fa-yen, "if you are carrying around a stone like that in your mind."

—ZEN STORY

We are here and
it is now. Further
than that, all human
knowledge is
moonshine.

—H. L. MENCKEN

Only *This, This!*

—SŌEN

I like reality. It tastes of bread.

—JEAN ANOUILH

A painting of a rice cake does not satisfy hunger.

—ANCIENT SAYING

When you ride in a boat and watch the shore, you might assume that the shore is moving. But when you keep your eyes closely on the boat, you can see that the boat moves. Similarly, if you examine many things with a confused mind, you might suppose that your mind and nature are permanent. But when you practice intimately and return to where you are, it will be clear that there is nothing that has an unchanging self.

—DŌGEN

Empty-handed, holding a hoe,

Walking, riding a water buffalo.

Man is crossing a bridge;

The bridge but not the river flows.

—MAHASATTVA FU

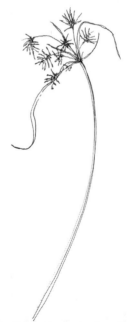

Two monks were arguing about the temple flag waving in the wind. One said, "The flag moves." The other said, "The wind moves." They argued back and forth but could not agree. Hui-neng, the Sixth Patriarch, said: "Gentlemen! It is not the flag that moves. It is not the wind that moves. It is your mind that moves." The two monks were struck with awe.

—ZEN KOAN

When you meet a master swordsman,

show him your sword.

When you meet a man who is not

   a poet,

Do not show him your poem.

—LIN-CHI

Zen in the Art of Archery and Swordsmanship

In his classic account *Zen in the Art of Archery* the German philosopher Eugen Herrigal sought Zen's marrow in the training of an archer—to discover where art becomes artless, shooting becomes not-shooting, and the archer becomes the target. "'I'm afraid I don't understand anything any more at all,' I answered, 'even the simplest things have got in a muddle. Is it "I" who draws the bow, or is it the bow that draws me . . . ? Do "I" hit the goal, or does the goal hit me? . . . Bow, arrow, goal and ego, all melt into one another, so that I can no longer separate them. And even the need to separate has gone. For as soon as I take the bow and shoot, everything becomes so clear and straightforward and so ridiculously simple. . . .'"

"'Now at last,' the Master broke in,

'The bowstring has cut right through you.'"

When pursued in the spirit of Zen, fencing, like archery, becomes a spiritual discipline. Zen Masters fence, and adepts of *kendo*—Japanese fencing—often train in Zen. It is another way of pursuing *mushin*, or "no-mindness." As the swordsman transcends the limits of his technique, putting aside all notions of displaying skill or winning a contest, the sword and the swordsman become one. Thoughts and feelings drop away as the swordsman returns to his "original mind."

Fundamentally the marksman aims at himself.

—*ZEN IN THE ART OF ARCHERY*

Should you desire the great tranquility, prepare to sweat white beads.

—HAKUIN

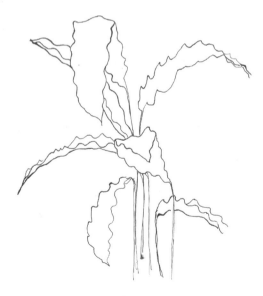

Awakening is indeed close
by—and supreme effort
is required to realize it.
Awakening is indeed
far away—and readily
accessible.

—STEPHEN BATCHELOR

Who are you in the silence between your thoughts?

—GIL FRONSDAL

The reason angels can fly is that they take themselves so lightly.

—G. K. CHESTERTON

Must it be?

It must be.

—BEETHOVEN

I can't go on.
You must go on.
I'll go on.

—SAMUEL BECKETT

It is like a water buffalo passing through a window. Its head, horns and four legs all pass through. Why can't its tail pass through, too?

—ZEN KOAN

When the way comes to an end, then change—having changed, you pass through.

—*I CHING*

And do not change. Do not divert your love from visible things. But go on loving what is good, simple and ordinary; animals and things and flowers, and keep the balance true.

—RAINER MARIA RILKE

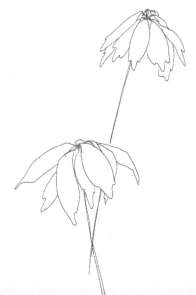

Knock,

And He'll open the door.

Vanish,

And He'll make you shine like the sun.

Fall,

And He'll raise you to the heavens.

Become nothing,

And He'll turn you into everything.

—RUMI

Everything is based on mind, is led by
mind, is fashioned by mind. If you speak
and act with a polluted mind, suffering
will follow you, as the wheels of the
oxcart follow the footsteps of the ox.
Everything is based on mind, is led by
mind, is fashioned by mind. If you speak
and act with a pure mind, happiness
will follow you, as a shadow clings to
a form.

—THE BUDDHA

There is nothing
either good or bad but
thinking makes it so.

—WILLIAM SHAKESPEARE

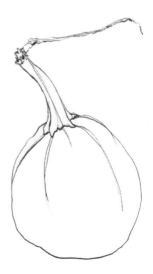

We try to evade the question [of existence] with property, prestige, power, production, fun, and, ultimately, by trying to forget that we—that I— exist. No matter how often he thinks of God or goes to church, or how much he believes in religious ideas, if he, the whole man, is deaf to the question of existence, if he does not have an answer to it, he is marking time, and he lives and dies like one of the million things he produces. He thinks of God, instead of experiencing God.

—ERICH FROMM

How refreshing, the whinny of a packhorse unloaded of everything!

—ZEN SAYING

Pai-chang wished to send a monk
to open a new monastery. He told
his pupils that whoever answered a
question most ably would be appointed.
Placing a water jug on the ground,
he asked: "Who can say what this is
without calling its name?"

The head monk said: "No one can call
it a wooden sandal."

Kuei-shan, the cooking monk, tipped
over the jug with his foot and went out.

Pai-chang laughed and said:
"The head monk loses."

And Kuei-shan became the Master of
the new monastery.

—ZEN MONDO

I AM THAT I AM.

—OLD TESTAMENT KOAN

What is the sound of one hand clapping?

—ZEN KOAN

Bind space with a rope and bring it to me.

—ZEN KOAN

Blow out a light a thousand miles away.

—ZEN KOAN

Who is he that is hearing at this very moment?

—BASSUI'S KOAN

Yen-kuan: Bring me the rhinoceros fan.

Attendant: It is broken.

Yen-kuan: In that case, bring me the rhinoceros.

The attendant couldn't answer.

—ZEN KOAN

Attachment is the great fabricator of illusions; reality can be attained only by someone who is detached.

—SIMONE WEIL

Two monks were once traveling together down a muddy road. A heavy rain was falling. Coming around the bend, they met a lovely girl in a silk kimono and sash, unable to cross the intersection.

"Come on, girl," said the first monk. Lifting her in his arms, he carried her over the mud.

The second monk did not speak again until that night when they reached a lodging temple. Then he no longer could restrain himself. "We monks don't go near females," he said. "It is dangerous. Why did you do that?"

"I left the girl there," the first monk said. "Are you still carrying her?"

—ZEN STORY

Wealthy patrons invited Ikkyū to a banquet. Ikkyū arrived dressed in his beggar's robes. The host, not recognizing him, chased him away. Ikkyū went home, changed into his ceremonial robe of purple brocade, and returned. With great respect, he was received into the banquet room. There, he put his robe on the cushion, saying, "I expect you invited the robe since you showed me away a little while ago," and left.

—ZEN STORY

Man's main task in life is to give birth to himself.

—ERICH FROMM

You must concentrate
upon and consecrate
yourself wholly to
each day, as though
a fire were raging in
your hair.

—DESHIMARU

It is reported that just before she died, Gertrude Stein asked: "What is the answer?" No answer came, and she laughed and said, "In that case, what is the question?" Then she died.

—WESTERN KOAN

Talking about Zen all the time is like looking for fish tracks in a dry riverbed.

—WU-TZU

Reading about enlightenment is like scratching an itch through your shoe.

—PHILIP KAPLEAU

Our own life is the instrument with which we experiment with truth.

—THICH NHAT HANH

One day Chuang-tzu and a friend were walking along a riverbank.

"How delightfully the fishes are enjoying themselves in the water!" Chuang-tzu exclaimed.

"You are not a fish," his friend said. "How do you know whether or not the fishes are enjoying themselves?"

"You are not me," Chuang-tzu said. "How do you know that I do not know that the fishes are enjoying themselves?"

—TAOIST MONDO

"My feet are cold,"
one man says, and the
legless man replies:
"So are mine. So are
mine."

—KENTUCKY FOLKLORE

Our goal should be to live life
in radical amazement . . . get
up in the morning and look
at the world in a way that
takes nothing for granted.
Everything is phenomenal. . . .
To be spiritual is to be amazed.

—ABRAHAM JOSHUA HESCHEL

Not knowing how near the truth is, we seek it far away.

—HAKUIN

The more you know
the less you understand.

—*TAO TE CHING*

A monk was anxious to learn Zen and said: "I have been newly initiated into the Brotherhood. Will you be gracious enough to show me the way to Zen?"

The Master said: "Do you hear the murmuring sound of the mountain stream?"

The monk said: "Yes, I do."

The Master said: "Here is the entrance."

—ZEN MONDO

Credits

For permission to use copyrighted or protected material, we thank the following literary executors and publishers. We have made every effort to obtain permission for reprint material in this book and to publish proper acknowledgments. We regret any error or oversight.

page iii: "Study of Two Pears," from *The Collected Poems of Wallace Stevens* by Wallace Stevens, copyright © 1954 by Wallace Stevens and copyright renewed 1982 by Holly Stevens. Used by permission of Alfred A. Knopf, an imprint of the Knopf Doubleday Publishing Group, a division of Penguin Random House LLC. All rights reserved. • pages 11, 98, 160, 181, 262, and 359: *Tao Te Ching: A New English Version* by Stephen Mitchell. Translation copyright © 1988 by Stephen Mitchell. Reprinted by permission of HarperCollins Publishers. • page 13: *Zen and the Birds of Appetite* by Thomas Merton. Copyright © 1968 by The Abbey of Gethsemani, Inc. Reprinted by permission of New Directions Publishing Corp. • page 31: "Anthem" by Leonard Cohen. From *Stranger Music* by Leonard Cohen. Copyright © 1993 Leonard Cohen and Leonard Cohen Stranger Music, Inc., used by permission of The Wylie Agency LLC. • page 32: *Pilgrim at Tinker Creek* by Annie Dillard. Copyright © 1974 by Annie Dillard. Reprinted by permission of HarperCollins Publishers. • pages 34, 92: *Teachings of the Buddha*, edited by Jack Kornfield and Gil Fronsdal. Copyright © 1993 by Jack Kornfield. Reprinted by arrangement with Shambhala Publications, Inc., 300 Massachusetts Avenue, Boston, MA 02115. • pages 35, 244, 297: *Zen and the Art of Motorcycle Maintenance* by Robert M. Pirsig. Copyright © 1974 by Robert M. Pirsig. Reprinted by permission of William Morrow and Company, Inc. • page 38: Three lines of "Stars" from *The Seven Ages* by Louise Glück. Copyright © 2001 by Louise Glück. Used by permission of HarperCollins Publishers. "Stars" first published in *The Seven Ages* and later collected in *Poems 1962–2012* by Louise Glück. Copyright © 2012 by Louise Glück, used by permission of The Wylie Agency LLC. • page 42: Quotation by Gertude Stein. Reprinted by permission of the Estate of Gertrude Stein by Calman A.

credits

Levin, Esq. • page 51: *A Man of Zen*, translated by Ruth Fuller Sasaki, Yoshitaka Iriya, and Dana Fraser. First edition, 1971. Published by Weatherhill, Inc., and reprinted by permission of the publisher. • pages 54–55: *A Glimpse of Nothingness* by Janwillem van de Wetering. Copyright © 1975 by Janwillem van de Wetering. Reprinted by permission of Houghton Mifflin Company. All rights reserved. • page 63: *The Way of Chuang Tzu* by Thomas Merton. Copyright © 1965 by The Abbey of Gethsemani, Inc. Reprinted by permission of New Directions Publishing Corp. • page 68: "Black Maps" from *Selected Poems* by Mark Strand, copyright © 1979, 1980 by Mark Strand. Used by permission of Alfred A. Knopf, an imprint of the Knopf Doubleday Publishing Group, a division of Penguin Random House LLC. All rights reserved. • page 82: *Herakleitos & Diogenes*, translated from the Greek by Guy Davenport. Copyright © 1979 by Guy Davenport. Reprinted by permission of Grey Fox Press. • pages 100, 143, 187, 219, 229: Haiku by Bashō, Buson, Issa, and Ryōkan from *Haiku: Volume One: Eastern Culture* by R. H. Blyth. Copyright © 1949, 1981 by The Hokuseido Press, used by permission of The Hokuseido Press. • page 113: *Ring of Bone* by Lew Welch, edited by Donald Allen. Copyright © 1979 by Grey Fox Press. Reprinted by permission of the publisher. • pages 115, 125, 149, 284, 285: Excerpts from Ta-hui Tsung-kao, Tessho, Issa, and Masahide from *The Penguin Book of Zen Poetry* edited and translated by Lucien Stryk and Takashi Ikemoto. Copyright © 1977 by Lucien Stryk and Takashi Ikemoto. Reprinted by permission of Penguin Books Ltd. • page 116: *Earth House Hold* by Gary Snyder. Copyright © 1969 by Gary Snyder. Reprinted by permission of New Directions Publishing Corp. • page 120: *Crow with No Mouth: Ikkyū, 15th Century Zen Master*. Copyright © 1989 by Stephen Berg. Reprinted by permission of Copper Canyon Press, P.O. Box 271, Port Townsend, WA 98368. • page 135: *The Dhammapada: The Sayings of the Buddha* by Thomas Byrom, translator. Copyright © 1976 by Thomas Byrom. Reprinted by permission of Alfred A. Knopf, Inc. • page 161: "Cold Mountain Poem #19" from *Riprap and Cold Mountain Poems* by Gary Snyder. Copyright © 1965 by Gary Snyder. Reprinted by permission of North Point Press, a division of Farrar, Straus & Giroux, Inc. • page 164: *The Bankei Zen* by Bankei. Reprinted by permission of Grove Weidenfield. • page 188: *The*

Way of Zen by Alan Watts. Copyright © 1957 by Pantheon Books, Inc. Reprinted by permission of Pantheon Books, a division of Random House, Inc. • page 189: *Moon in a Dewdrop: Writings of Zen Master Dōgen*, edited by Kazuaki Tanahashi. Copyright © 1985 by the San Francisco Zen Center. Reprinted by permission of North Point Press, a division of Farrar, Straus & Giroux, Inc. • pages 198, 293: Excerpts by Dōgen from *The Enlightened Mind*, edited by Stephen Mitchell. Copyright © 1991 by Stephen Mitchell. Reprinted by permission of HarperCollins Publishers. • page 200: *Dewdrops on a Lotus Leaf: Zen Poems by Ryōkan*, translated by John Stevens. Copyright © 1993 by John Stevens. Reprinted by arrangement with Shambhala Publications, Inc., 300 Massachusetts Avenue, Boston, MA 02115. • page 203: *Zen: Poems, Prayers, Sermons, Anecdotes, Interviews* by Lucien Stryk, ed. Translated by Takashi Ikemoto. Copyright © 1965 by Lucien Stryk and Takashi Ikemoto. Used by permission of Doubleday, a division of Bantam Doubleday Dell Publishing Group, Inc. • page 207: *Zen Buddhism and Psychoanalysis*. Reprinted by permission of HarperCollins Publishers. • page 208: Five lines of "Ahimsa ('Returning to the Country for a Brief Visit')" from *Collected Poems 1947/1997* by Allen Ginsberg. Copyright © 2006 by the Allen Ginsberg Trust. Used by permission of HarperCollins Publishers. "Returning to the Country for a Brief Visit" by Allen Ginsberg, currently collected in *Collected Poems 1947/1997*. Copyright © 1973 by Allen Ginsberg, used by permission of The Wylie Agency LLC. • page 210: *Zen and Japanese Culture* by D. T. Suzuki. Copyright © 1959 by Bollingen Foundation, Inc., New York, NY. Reprinted by permission of Princeton University Press. • page 213: *Triumph of the Sparrow: Zen Poems of Shinkichi Takahashi* translated by Lucien Stryk copyright © 1986 by Lucien Stryk. Used by permission of Grove/Atlantic, Inc. • page 217: "To Make a Prairie" (1755) by Emily Dickinson, from *The Poems of Emily Dickinson* edited by Thomas H. Johnson, Cambridge, Mass.: The Belknap Press of Harvard University Press, Copyright © 1951, 1955, 1979, 1983 by the President and Fellows of Harvard College. • page 225: *Goodnight Moon* by Margaret Wise Brown. Copyright © 1947 by Margaret Wise Brown. Reprinted by permission of HarperCollins Publishers. • page 270: "Fourth Meditation" by Theodore Roethke. Copyright © 1966 and renewed 1994

ACKNOWLEDGMENTS

With special thanks to Janet Vicario, for her visual partnership;
Mary Ellen O'Neill, for her insights and enthusiasm;
Suzie Bolotin and Page Edmunds,
for making this project happen;
and Lia Ronnen, for her invaluable support.

DAVID SCHILLER

is an author and artist whose previous
books include *See Your Way to Mindfulness,*
The Little Book of Prayers, and *Guitar.*
Follow him on Instagram @openyouri
and online at davidschiller.com.

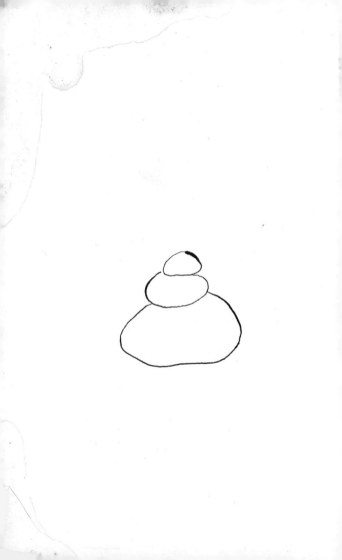